YOUR KNOWLEDGE HAS VALUE

- We will publish your bachelor's and master's thesis, essays and papers

- Your own eBook and book - sold worldwide in all relevant shops

- Earn money with each sale

Upload your text at www.GRIN.com
and publish for free

Bibliographic information published by the German National Library:

The German National Library lists this publication in the National Bibliography; detailed bibliographic data are available on the Internet at http://dnb.dnb.de .

Imprint:

Copyright © 2018 GRIN Verlag
Print and binding: Books on Demand GmbH, Norderstedt Germany
ISBN: 9783668873681

This book at GRIN:

https://www.grin.com/document/457710

Paulina Pietsch

Trust and Betrayal. The Motive of Friendship in Hamlet

GRIN Verlag

GRIN - Your knowledge has value

Since its foundation in 1998, GRIN has specialized in publishing academic texts by students, college teachers and other academics as e-book and printed book. The website www.grin.com is an ideal platform for presenting term papers, final papers, scientific essays, dissertations and specialist books.

Visit us on the internet:

http://www.grin.com/

http://www.facebook.com/grincom

http://www.twitter.com/grin_com

Qualifikationsjahrgang 2017/2019

Seminararbeit

Wissenschaftspropädeutisches Seminar im Fach Englisch

"Trust and Betrayal - The Motive of Friendship in Hamlet"

Verfasser: Paulina Pietsch

Abgabetermin: 06.11.2018

Contents

1 Introduction

A son revenges the murder of his father. This is the briefest description of the plot of *Hamlet*, one of Shakespeare's best-known plays. However, the tragedy explores many more ideas than just revenge, including death, love, family, politics, deception, the meaning of life, the impossibility of certainty, the complexity of action, the abilities of drama, misogyny, madness, religion, competing worldviews, loyalty, sex, gender and friendship. Even though friendship is one of the most important parts of everyone's life, it is often forgotten about when summing up one of Shakespeare's tragedies. The theme of friendship, with the exception of *Timon of Athens*, often seems to be secondary. The first associations with *Romeo and Juliet* are forbidden love and tragic death, with *Macbeth* they are madness and ambition, with *Othello* they are love and prejudices, and with *Hamlet* they are revenge, madness and lies.

However, the theme of friendship must have been somehow essential to William Shakespeare, since he completely invented a friend not only for dramatic purposes but also for moral support for his tragic hero. The origin of the characters Horatio, Rosencrantz and Guildenstern and their roles in the play *Hamlet* will be examined later. Furthermore, this paper aims to put the often-forgotten motive of friendship in *Hamlet*, Shakespeare's longest play and one of the most powerful and influential works of world literature, in the spotlight. It will give an overview of the Elizabethan understanding of friendship, portray Horatio's and Hamlet's friendship, examine the possible reasons for Rosencrantz's and Guildenstern's betrayal – both are former friends of Hamlet - and answer the question how similar these friendships are to modern ones.

2 Shakespeare's Sources

Like most dramatists of his time, Shakespeare did not invent the main plots of his plays but instead adapted them. The story of *Hamlet* derives from the legend of Amleth, preserved by Saxo Grammaticus in *Amlethus* and retold by François de Belleforest in *XVII Histoires Tragiques*. Shakespeare may also have used a now lost earlier Elizabethan play known as *The Ur-Hamlet* by Thomas Kyd.

In Saxo Grammaticus' *Amlethus*, the character closest to Horatio, Hamlet's loyal friend, can be found. A 'milk brother' of Amleth (21) appears as his warner and adviser, e.g. when, by seduction by a woman, Amleth is to be tested whether he is crazy or pretends to be (19ff). Since the milk brother's strange warning, to attach chaff to the tail of a horsefly that flies to Amleth (25), was invented because of an Old Norse pun that Saxo could not recognise anymore (4), it cannot be used for concluding about his character. Since he is mentioned only on this occasion, he does not gain a firm shape, although a certain personal relationship with Amleth is implied. In the Saxo-dependent Hamlet story of the *XVII Histoires Tragiques* by Belleforest, this 'milk brother' remains even paler and less substantial than in *Amlethus* and it is unknown if Thomas Kyd's lost play known as *The Ur-Hamlet* featured a friend of Hamlet. However, in his *Spanish Tragedy*, a friend of Andrea called 'Horatio' can be found. Considering the way Thomas Kyd portrays their friendship, it becomes clear that Shakespeare only took over the name. Kyd makes Horatio fall in love with Bel-Imperia (see II.2), Andrea's lover, making every kind of friendship between Horatio and Andrea impossible. It is obvious that Shakespeare found only a little inspiration for his Horatio these sources and, inspired by Orestes and Pylades, made him into an intellectual and moral companion with whom Hamlet can share secrets and discuss philosophy. For Herbert Burre, Horatio is Hamlet's "mirror of normality" (see 37), for G. F. Bradby, on the other hand, Horatio has "no very marked individuality" (15), and for John Dover Wilson he is "a piece of dramatic structure" (235). However, only because he "give[s] the audience necessary information about the political situation in Denmark" (235) and "is the recipient of information even more necessary for the audience to hear" (235), it does not mean that he can merely be reduced to a structure. Maybe Bradby and Wilson came to those conclusions because Horatio has relatively low speaking shares. With only 265 spoken lines[1], he does not appear very impactful. However, what Horatio does and says is essential and the

---

[1] Of the male protagonists, only Laertes has less spoken lines.

detailed account of his friendship with Hamlet shows that Horatio is not merely a scheme, but a genuine Shakespearean figure.

For the characters of Rosencrantz and Guildenstern, an initial version can be found in *Amlethus* and the *XVII Histoires Tragiques*. Saxo describes them in a similar way to Belleforest as two followers of Fenge who accompany Amlethus on the journey to England carrying a message ordering the King of England to kill the boy sent to him (see 35). Just like Rosencrantz and Guildenstern, they die because Amlethus finds the message and exchanges his name for those of his escorts (see 35). However, Shakespeare fully developed their characters. The two escorts now have Danish aristocratic sixteenth-century names ("Rosenkrantz", "Gyldenstierne"), a detailed history of their prior friendship with Hamlet, ambitions to serve the new King and the task to bring, due to their duality (see Metzler 42), comic relief to the audience. As a result, the play features more contrasts, parallels and interactions of related plot lines than in Shakespeare's sources.

3 Elizabethan Friendship

Since *Hamlet* is a play written by an Elizabethan for Elizabethans, one has to consider their ideas of friendship before trying to understand how Shakespeare processed this topic in the play. Will Tosh explains in his article *Shakespeare and friendship* that Shakespeare used the term 'friend' as it is used nowadays when meaning a familiar companion, but also when meaning other kinds of relations, e.g. family members, lovers or neighbours. In the broadest sense, a friend was "one's fellow subject". In contrast to this equivocal definition, friendship was seen as something "very much deeper and more significant" than it is today. As Tosh writes: "For some, friendship was a preciously rare union of profound emotional, intellectual, spiritual and physical intensity, experienced by a lucky few and impossible to resist". Friendship being described with such an intensity and vocabulary, which would nowadays be associated with romantic or sexual love, causes a blurring of lines. Some same-sex friendships were intense but platonic, for others the intimacy of same-sex friendship provided a context within which homosexual desire could be explored and expressed, especially in a period when same-sex sexual relationships were disapproved. However, since the latter were concealed, friendship was raised above marriage in people's minds being free of "the sin of sexuality". According to Michel de Montaigne, a philosopher of the French Renaissance, the friends' "souls are mingled and confounded in so universal a blending that they efface the seam which joins them together so that it cannot be found" (9) in the perfect kind of friendship. Then, "each gives himself so entirely to his friend that he has nothing left to share with another" (15). The Roman politician and philosopher Marcus Tullius Cicero uses in *On Living and Dying Well* similar metaphors when praising a friend as "another self" (100) and the process of becoming friends as "several souls becom[ing] ... one" (104).

Many male writers, e.g. Montaigne and Aristotle, held the male friendship particularly in high esteem, assuming only men were capable of resisting the powerful emotions of friendship (Montaigne 7). Aristotle believed that the perfect friendship could only exist "between good men" (206) and Will Tosh states that even treatises defined friendship "as something that only existed in its ideal form between men of similar intellect, moral courage and ethical firmness". He sees this misogynistic sense portrayed in George Wither's emblem for friendship. It shows

Illustration 1: George Wither's emblem for friendship

a pair of clasped hands holding a crowned and flaming heart, circled with linked rings. The Latin words 'bona fide' around the engraving mean 'with good faith'. Although Tosh states the illustration shows "two male hands", he gives no proof or an explanation why he came to that conclusion. The verses above and below the engraving never mention any gender, but describe friendship as a 'true-love' of dependability, mutuality and generosity existing in the time of need. However, Tosh has a point when referring to the Elizabethan education as a reason for the misogyny. Since all of the examples of ideal friends, e.g. Orestes and Pylades, Damon and Pythias, David and Jonathan, Elizabethans were taught to admire, were men.

4   The Motive of Friendship in Hamlet

4.1   Hamlet's Trust in Horatio

Hamlet, like anybody belonging to a royal family or having a position of extraordinary wealth or power, is facing the problem of having to sort out who is a true friend and who is a flatterer. At the beginning of the play, Hamlet shows his distrust in Horatio and Marcellus fearing they will reveal his secret. After Horatio and Marcellus both swore by heaven they would not, he starts telling them. However, Hamlet interrupts himself and finishes the sentence other than he probably first intended to, with 'like King Claudius' and keeps quiet about what the ghost told him.

> HAMLET.
> There's never a villain dwelling in all Denmark -
> But he's an arrant knave. (I.5.123-124)[2]

According to Wilson, Hamlet already knows he can trust Horatio and wants to tell him all, but first, he has to make sure that the other witness, Marcellus, keeps quiet (Wilson 78f). Horatio's words show that Hamlet's behaviour hurts him (I.5.133-135). Since Hamlet does not want to offend the only friend he has, he "takes him aside to tell him something of the truth" (Wilson 79, I.5.136-138). He nearly reveals the secret to Horatio, but when realising Marcellus is still present, he breaks off and instead goes back to addressing them both (I.5.139-141).

Another interpretation would be that Hamlet does precisely what one should do according to Cicero: "judge before loving, not love before judging" (101). Aristotle had a similar view on this topic stating that friends "need time and intimacy" (206) to get to know each other. According to him, a man could not "accept another, or the two become friends, until each has proved to the other that he is worthy of love and so has won his trust" (206). Hamlet gets this proof when Horatio helps him determine the guilt of the King (III.2.88-99). Horatio has the important task of observing Claudius' reactions during the play within the play, being Hamlet's accomplice, his second pair of eyes and of seeing everything Hamlet misses.

In IV.6 Hamlet addresses himself in his letter to Horatio as "he that thou knowest thine" (IV.6.30) showing his devotion towards Horatio. However, he does not tell his friend about the conversation with the ghost until V.2. Here, the prince finally tells Horatio the secret (V.2.64-67) he has kept from him for such a long time. Hamlet has difficulty with not knowing whom

---

[2] All following quotes provided with this kind of parenthetical citation refer to the play *Hamlet*.

to trust and whom to ask for advice: Ophelia returned his love letters, the relationship is over. Furthermore, he is disgusted by his mother's behaviour, he is distressed about his father having been murdered by his uncle, he sees himself surrounded by political corruption, intrigue, and betrayal by his former close friends Rosencrantz and Guildenstern and he does not know what he is supposed to do about it. But in Horatio he finds a good friend who is the only one on whom he can rely wholeheartedly.

4.2   Horatio's Qualities as a Friend

Horatio shows his most beautiful qualities as a friend in recognising and respecting Hamlet's peculiarity. Even though he does not entirely understand his friend's odd behaviour, he never judges him once in the play. His caring for Hamlet can be seen in I.4 where Horatio begs Hamlet not to follow the ghost. However, Hamlet does not listen to him. In V.2, Hamlet is challenged to a duel by Laertes. Horatio notices that the prince only pretends to be strong when predicting Hamlet would lose the bet (V.2.203). After Hamlet's comment "Thou wouldst not think how ill all's here about my heart" (V.2.206f), Horatio tries to stop him from participating in the duel and offers to make up excuses for Hamlet. He does not let us doubt for a moment about the bond between him and Hamlet by being exactly the friend that Hamlet needs. A friend with that unwavering strength and stability of character who gives security and calmness simply through his mere presence and occasional word (III.2.295, III.3.301). He wishes the best for his friend's (Aristotle 205) and not for his own sake and loves Hamlet the way he is. This behaviour was classified by Aristotle as the correct behaviour in the "perfect friendship based on goodness" (205).

On the other hand, Horatio does not fear to disagree and argue with the prince and even criticise him for his doing. When Hamlet tells him about his plot on Rosencrantz and Guildenstern, Horatio's "So Rosencrantz and Guildenstern go to it" (V.2.55) is a quiet, but no less significant, reproach on the brutality of the deed. He proves that his loyalty has nothing to do with uncritical devotion by following Cicero's guideline "giving and taking criticism is the mark of a true friendship" (103). Although the friendship with Horatio may remain Hamlet's only, sincere and stable feeling of solidarity until the end, even Horatio as his closest confidant can never win a determining influence on his actions and thinking.

4.3   Equality in Hamlet's and Horatio's Friendship

Horatio's ability to criticise Hamlet (V.2.55) and to argue with him (I.5.166f) is one of the most significant signs showing they have an exceptional kind of friendship where they trust and love each other, while at the same time still enjoy their diversity. Opposite to Cicero's thesis "full agreement" (80) being "the essence of friendship" (80), they are trying to persuade each other and therefore, learn how to be open to suggestion, but also how to hold on to their position. Most important is that when they are having a discussion, it nearly does not matter that Hamlet is the prince of Denmark and has a much higher rank than Horatio. They forget about it because they feel equal which is one of the essential aspects of a lasting friendship. Horatio, due to his mental abilities and knowledge, is the centre of conversation when accompanied by Marcellus and Bernardo. However, when accompanied by Hamlet, he tends to subordinate by calling himself a "servant" (I.2.162) or Hamlet his "lord" (I.2., III.2.63, V.1.80, V.1.), behaving properly towards a superior and showing his inner nobility and modesty. Hamlet, on the other hand, also behaves correctly according to Cicero and treats a friend of lower rank as an equal (97) by calling him "good friend" (I.2.163) and "fellow-student" (I.2.177). Horatio understands Hamlet's offer correctly, but he still preserves the formality knowing that warmth can exist even if a particular form is maintained. Aristotle explains in his *Nicomachean Ethics* the importance of equality in a friendship (209-213). According to him, people in high positions tend to have friends who are either useful to them or agreeable.

> We have said that the good man is also both useful and agreeable, but such a person does not become the friend of a superior in rank unless the latter is his superior in goodness too. Otherwise the inferior cannot make a proportionately equal return. (Aristotle 211)

Horatio has to be the superior in goodness and have the right proportion of "blood and judgement" (III.2.79). Otherwise, the two would not be as good friends as they are. Proof for this thesis is Hamlet's declaration of love to Horatio in III.2. Horatio is not "passion's slave" (III.2.82) like Hamlet who completely loses his self-control when Ophelia gives him back his love letters (III.1.93-150) or when he talks to his mother and ends up killing Polonius (III.4.9-103). The diversity of their natures becomes clear again in the cemetery scene in V.1. The labile Hamlet deeply impressed by the atmosphere of the cemetery and the unemotional gravediggers, lets the game of his thoughts run wild. Again, as so often before, he faces the question of the nature of death. When he talks about Alexander's "noble dust" (V.1.200), Horatio again acts as the more reasonable part in their relationship by saying "'Twere to consider too curiously to consider so" (V.1.202).

4.4   Hamlet, Horatio and the Ghost

Horatio comes across as a scientist, as an inductive person, as a character wanting evidence. The best proof of this thesis is to be found in I.1 where Horatio is invited by members of the guard to speak to a ghost, they have seen.

> MARCELLUS.
> Thou art a scholar. Speak to it, Horatio. (I.1.41)

The soldiers have seen a ghost resembling the dead King Hamlet, the prince's father, two nights in a row and are afraid of the whole situation.

> HORATIO.
> Tush, tush, 'twill not appear. (I.1.30)
> Before my God, I might not this believe
> Without the sensible and true avouch
> Of mine own eyes. (I.1.56-58)

Horatio's response shows his incredulity. David Bevington, an American literary scholar, compares Horatio's behaviour to Thomas', one of the twelve disciples, after the resurrection of Christ.

> So the other disciples told him, "We have seen the Lord!"
> But he said to them, "Unless I see the nail marks in his hands and put my
> finger where the nails were, and put my hand into his side, I will not
> believe." (New International Version, Jn. 20.25)

Thomas can believe in the impossible and unseen, but only after he saw and touched Christ, like Horatio who starts believing after seeing the ghost. For a moment, he is not the enlightened sceptic anymore, pale and trembling as he is (I.1.53). The supernatural phenomenon shakes his rational beliefs and, in his need, to understand it, his modern rational protestant thinking knows no other advice than to fall back on the old medieval model of the world. He interprets the ghost as a bad omen, which "bodes some strange eruption to our state" (I.1.69). Thus, the return of a royal dead man can point out a fundamental disturbance in the order of the divine hierarchical macrocosm and may mean chaos for the order of the state, as it did in Rome before the murder of Caesar. He recalls how, according to tradition, there were signs of supernaturalism in Rome, e.g. fierce comets, walking dead and lunar eclipses, which pointed to an approaching fatality (I.1.80-125). Confusion and difficulties in interpreting the happenings result in Horatio resorting to the certainties of the past, and he suddenly delivers a Catholic interpretation of the spirit. The play immediately introduces the topic of competing world interpretations: The guards believe in the spirit; the sceptic Horatio still believes in it being an "illusion" (I.1.128). It is by no means a coincidence that Horatio is a student from the enlightened Lutheran-Protestant University of Wittenberg. With this location, Shakespeare places his work in the context of the great upheaval in Western ideas and the Reformation which had shaken the orderly theocentric view of the world. Right from the start, the play is crossing the balance between faith and reasonable investigation, and it is crucial to have Horatio fill the role of the sceptic in contrast to Hamlet's mentality.

HAMLET.
>   There are more things in heaven and in earth, Horatio,
>   Than are dreamt of in your philosophy. (I.5.166-167)

Hamlet himself also does not know what to believe, although his doubts about the ghost do not concern its objectivity. As Wilson ascertains, he never shows any sign of hesitation or disbelief (see 71). Other than Horatio, Hamlet doubts "the identity of the Ghost and the nature of the place from which it comes" (Wilson 71). He does not know whether this ghost is his father's spirit or whether it is another supernatural creature, e.g. a devil or an angel.

HAMLET.
>   If it assume my noble father's person,
>   I'll speak to it, though hell itself should gape
>   And bid me hold my peace. (I.2.244-246)

His use of the word 'assume' implies that the spirit could be masquerading as the late King while his reference to "hell itself" (I.2.245) implies the possibility that it could be demonic in origin. The following line "My father's spirit! In arms! All is not well." (I.2.255) could be interpreted as the recognition of the possibility it is his father, of a possibility he would undoubtedly love to believe, but is too smart to accept. This ambivalence becomes more apparent as the play progresses. When meeting the spirit, he again expresses "his theological prepossessions" (Wilson 71, I.4.39-45), but the conversation with the spirit seems to convince him entirely that it is his father's. His doubts are laid to rest after staging the play within the play to proof Claudius' guilt (II.2.596-601) and therefore whether the ghost told the truth. Now Hamlet can "take the ghost's words for a thousand pound" (III.2.295f)

4.5   Hamlet's and Horatio's Mentality

Before the play within the play, Hamlet explains to Horatio that he has chosen him as his friend, because he is the most honourable man he has ever met (III.2.64-65). In deep excitement, which is linguistically expressed by the "thou" Hamlet uses from now on, he recognizes Horatio as the "just man," who takes "Fortune's buffets and rewards ... with equal thanks" (III.2.77f) and has the right proportion of "blood and judgment" (III.2.79) that Hamlet does not have despite his richer nature. This speech in praise of Horatio's nature could be described as a thumbnail sketch of stoicism. In the introduction of *Hamlet*, Alan Sinfield defines the stoic outlook: "one must accept with tranquillity those forces one cannot control" (xxxi)[3]. No mystery could disturb him emotionally that is why he sees natural events such as death not as dreadful or scary.

---

[3] Quotes provided with this kind of parenthetical citation refer to an introduction.

Hamlet on the other side turns out to be a Christian whose belief in heaven and hell is problematic in certain ways. A good example can be found in III.3 after the play within the play. When Hamlet comes across the King at prayer, Claudius is failing to pray because he is unwilling to give up the effects for which he committed the murder (see III.3.53-54). Hamlet's first intention is to use the opportunity and stab the King. However, he pauses and concludes that if he killed Claudius now, the King might go to heaven which is the opposite of Hamlet's goal (III.3.74-82). He decides to kill Claudius "When he is drunk sleep, or in his rage, / Or in th'incestuous pleasure of his bed, / At game, a-swearing, or about some act/ That has no relish of salvation in't" (III.3.90-92). This is the reason why he mistakenly stabs Polonius behind the arras in III.4. Hamlet comes to his mother's chambers to speak with her, but then he hears a man's voice in her room. Since he has been looking for an opportunity to kill Claudius when his soul is ripe for damnation, the King and his mother in her bedchamber sounds like the right moment. Hamlet stabs and kills the wrong man, realising he has made a mistake (III.4.25-33).

> HAMLET.
> For this same lord,
> I do repent. But heaven hath pleased it so,
> To punish me with this, and this with me (III.4.173-175)

Hamlet sees that he must bear the consequences of having killed the wrong person which is the meaning of "me with this" (III.4.175). "This with me" (III.4.175), means that Polonius has to pay for his meddling with the prince's life. Hamlet sees himself and his doing as determined through some providential plan which he cannot figure out. However, the solution comes to him as an event he had not called for or planned. He is challenged to a duel with Laertes in the presence of the King for entertainment. When Hamlet accepts the challenge, he knows nothing about Laertes meeting up with the King to cook up a plot to make sure Hamlet will be killed with a poisoned sword or if not with a backup cup of poisoned wine. Hamlet did not devise this, is not conspiring and not trying to work out how to get the King killed. In the duel, Hamlet hits Laertes with the poisoned sword, and Claudius accidentally poisons his wife with the wine. It is almost a joke. For Hamlet this joke means that after having criticised himself for not knowing what to do, the answer comes to him by means that he could not have devised and has not devised himself. Him murdering Claudius is almost an act of self-defence. That is the providential reading of his own story, and it regards at the same time Christian theology. However, there is Horatio, his dear friend, whose first move with these terrifying last moments, of course, is wanting to kill himself.

> HORATIO.
> I am more an antique Roman than a Dane. (V.2.335)

This line can be interpreted in different ways. Either Horatio sees killing himself as self-evident and does not fear death, because for him it is a natural event or Horatio is for a moment not the one taking Fortune's buffets and rewards with equal thanks (III.2.77-78). He offers the greatest act of friendship by killing himself and uniting with Hamlet in death. Seeing it like a stoic model of suicide, he believes that when things have reached a certain point, there is just no remedy. However, Hamlet insists on Horatio to stay alive and tell his story (V.2.336-342). It leaves Horatio to explain what has happened to Fortinbras. His explanation is very different from Hamlet´s providential interpretation. According to Horatio, everything happened the way it did because "Of carnal, bloody, and unnatural acts. / Of accidental judgements, casual slaughters, / Of deaths put on by cunning and forced cause, / And … purposes mistook / Fallen on th'inventors' heads" (V.2.375-379). That is not a bad rating of many of the ingredients of Hamlet, but it is a secular Roman historical report having no room in it for a providential or Christian interpretation. Horatio sees the events as a story of people digging their graves and falling into things they justly deserve.

4.6 Rosencrantz' and Guildenstern's Betrayal

Rosencrantz and Guildenstern also knew Hamlet from school and have been his friends since his "young days" (II.2.11), and the Queen is sure that "two men there is not living / To whom he more adheres" (II.2.20-21). Indeed, Hamlet is overjoyed to see them, gives them a joyful, warm welcome, addresses them as his "excellent good friends" (II.2.224), and they obscenely joke together (II.2.228-235). They are his "friends of long standing" (Wilson 118) whose company he longs for because they are a distraction from his thoughts. He has not sorted out yet who are the right people to trust, so he tells them about his bad dreams and how Denmark feels like a prison to him (239-255). However, Hamlet quickly figures out that they were sent for due to their inability of believable lying (II.2.269-291). Guildenstern finally admits it after Hamlet's demand "If you love me, hold not off" (II.2.290-291). Even though they are acting as the King's agents, they conceal the fact that the prince unmasked them to Claudius.

Since they are the King's spies, it is easy to think of Rosencrantz and Guildenstern as terrible friends and traitors. If their behaviour is analysed with this thought in mind, they perfectly fit in Aristotle's description of friends of utility in his Nicomachean Ethics. They seem to not love Hamlet for his "personal qualities" (Aristotle 204) but only for the benefits they get out of his friendship, which are under the assumption that Claudius paid them for their services, prestige and wealth. For the Elizabethans who valued friendship as a rare, precious and passionate union and praised it as "the peak of perfection" (Montaigne 3) within the fellowship, this kind of false friendship would have been "the greatest of betrayals" (Tosh).

However, it is to say that, from Rosencrantz's and Guildenstern's point of view, they were brought down out of circumstances that are not self-evidently criminal or corrupted. The King and Queen had sent for them because they knew Hamlet when he was young and are in worry because of his recent strange behaviour (II.2.3-12). There is no good reason for finding that action morally repellent since the proposition is very reasonable. What would we say of Claudius and Gertrude as parents, if they took no effort in finding the reason for their son's distress? Moreover, what would we say of them as King and Queen, if they allowed madness to go unwatched? Since Rosencrantz and Guildenstern are not only loyal subjects but, as their later speeches on kingship remind us, also enthusiastic royalists awed by authority and thrilled by their contact with majesty. Their obedience towards the King can further be seen in III.3, shortly after the play within the play. Claudius tells Rosencrantz and Guildenstern about his worries, this time concerning his own life. He sees Hamlet as a security problem threatening his life, and since he is head of state, his life has to be protected at all costs. Of course, Rosencrantz and Guildenstern are immediately willing to do whatever Claudius asks for, in this case going to England with Hamlet (III.3.7-23).

> GUILDENSTERN.
> Most holy and religious fear it is
> To keep those many bodies safe
> That live and feed upon your majesty. (III.3.8-10)

What Rosencrantz and Guildenstern are saying to Claudius, is an entirely correct dogma in Elizabethan England. David Bevington states that in the Anglican Church, there were sermons against disobedience and rebellion, in other words, pieces of propaganda, that required to be read from time to time. According to him, the public dogma was that it is a matter of holy set and reverential need to protect the life of the head of state. Anybody who dared to threaten the King or the Queen was committing a crime against God as well as against the state which is what Hamlet does from their point of view. Also, Elizabethans believed very firmly that one should always be obedient to a monarch. To them, Claudius appears to be a competent administrator and a good politician. He handles the sensitive situation with a threatening invasion from Norway with great calmness and saves the situation. From Rosencrantz's and Guildenstern's point of view, they are merely acting as loyal subjects of their excellent King.

In Hamlet's eyes, they were never right in their love for him and have become agents of the King and Queen to spy on him. An excellent example for this can be found in III.2 after the play within the play where Hamlet uses the chance to make fun of Guildenstern. He explains to him the technique of playing the pipe which "is as easy as lying" (III.2.365) and compares covering the holes to covering the truth. Of course, playing the pipe is not as simple as Hamlet presents it which is what he is playing with. When Guildenstern answers "I cannot" (III.2.360), "I have not the skill" (III.2.370), Hamlet responds with the accusation that Guildenstern already played on him.

> HAMLET. Why, look now, how unworthy a thing you
> make of me! You would play upon me. (III.2.371-372)
> … 'Sblood, do you think I am easier to be played
> on than a pipe? Call me what instrument you will,
> though you can fret me, you cannot play upon me. (III.2.377-379)

He plays with the word 'fret' in the musical sense, but also 'fretting' in the sense of irritating. This metaphor is a beautiful illustration of their friendship and the reason he cannot trust them. When Rosencrantz and Guildenstern are assigned by the King to escort Hamlet to England, he describes them to his mother as his "two schoolfellows" (III.4.204) whom he will trust as he "will adders fanged" (III.4.205). Comparing his escorts to the viper, the only poisonous snake in Britain ("adder"), Hamlet makes his distrust very clear.

The problem, of course, is that they do not know that Claudius himself has murdered the former King, which would change everything. They are put in an interesting position because they are trying to be friends to Hamlet, but end up being on the other side. Like Eldridge Cleaver once said, "You either have to be part of the solution, or you're going to be part of the problem" and they cannot be part of the solution because Hamlet cannot trust them. On their voyage to England, he unseals a letter Rosencrantz and Guildenstern carry, learning that he is supposed to be executed. Hamlet changes his name for those of his false friends, escapes back to Denmark and lets Rosencrantz and Guildenstern find their reward (IV.6.13-30, V.2.48-62). With their characters of politeness and mediocrity, and in the blurring of any individual, they form a direct contrast to the friends Hamlet and Horatio. Rosencrantz and Guildenstern can dramatically only exit as a duo. They continuously stick together, feel connected in their absolute equality, in which no one has anything unique and individual. Even though their inclinations are good, they lack firm character patterns to follow them and cannot even practice villainy with success. "You were sent for," (II.2.278f) says Hamlet, "and there is a kind of confession in your looks, which your modesties have not craft enough to colour" (II.2.279f). They commit no actual crime in the play and are more fools than villains, but foolishness is often more harmful than villainy.

5 Conclusion

After the in-depth work on the friendship in Shakespeare's *Hamlet* there are two main conclusions to be drawn:

Firstly, to answer the question from the introduction, Shakespeare's and nowadays friendships follow the same ideals and are therefore similar in many aspects. The fact that Shakespeare presents the friendship between Hamlet and Horatio as, according to several philosophers, a perfect friendship, shows that he may have believed in the Elizabethan ideals explained in chapter 2. His characters and their relationships are timeless and realistic or as Allan Bloom phrased it: "Shakespeare seems to be the mirror of nature and to present human beings as they are." (1). Even though the friendships are based on Elizabethan beliefs, we can comprehend them easily because we still share parts of those beliefs. Besides the misogynist aspect, the ideal friend nowadays still is what Aristotle, Montaigne and Cicero described: a friend with whom everything can be shared, who loves one for who one is, who is by one's side in the time of need and who is not afraid to point out one's mistakes. However, those friends are hard to find and even harder to keep. In a time when friendships can be built faster via the internet, it is often forgotten that taking care of a friendship in order to keep it alive requires time and effort. Even though we can connect with people from the other side of the world, we miss the opportunity to keep close those friends we already have and who are already part of our lives.

Secondly, I have learned while working on this paper that Shakespeare's plays hide many pearls of wisdom of this kind and bear much more than is evident from the start. Just like *Hamlet* is not only about revenge, *Romeo and Juliet* is more about than only love. The problem with discovering these hidden treasures is that, since Shakespeare's language is more than 400 years old, one has to invest much time in observing, finding and understanding the different possible meanings and interpretations of his words. However, the time invested pays out, since one can learn a lot about one's life and relationships. Unfortunately, the majority of students has had bad experiences with Shakespeare in school because the language or meaning was not understood. The goal should be to get students excited about Shakespeare rather than discouraging them. Therefore, the way in which this topic is approached in class must be improved. Because his plays are not just literary texts but working scripts, they require collaboration, voice, and movement. "Choral readings, comparative viewing, quartos and folios, tableaux vivant, speaking text and subtext, writing directorial commentary, blocking scenes—these and other reading, writing, and performance strategies empower students to explore language with their whole bodies" (Daken xv). These texts should be treated more as dramas which are meant to be enacted and not to be read bored in a classroom.

6 Bibliography

6.1 Primary Sources

Aristoteles; Thompson; et al. *The Nicomachean Ethics*. 1961. Trans. J. A. K. Penguin Classics. London: Penguin Books, 2004.

Bandello, Matteo ; Belleforest, Francois de ; Boaistuau, Pierre. *XVII Histoires tragiques*. n.p.: 1560.

Cicero, Marcus Tullius. *On Living and Dying Well*. Trans. Thomas Habinek. Penguin Classics. London: Penguin Books, 2012.

Grammaticus, Saxo. *Amlethus*. Trans. Gerhart Sieveking. Introduction by Gerhart Sieveking. Hamburg: Gesellschaft der Bücherfreunde, 1947.

Kyd, Thomas. *The Spanish Tragedy: A Norton Critical Edition*. Edited by Michael Neill. London: W.W. Norton & Company, 2014.

Montaigne, Michel de. *On Friendship*. 1991. Penguin Classics. New York: Penguin Books, 2005. 1-21

Shakespeare, William. *Hamlet*. 1980. Ed. T. B. J. Spencer. Introduction by Alan Sinfield. Penguin Classics. London: Penguin Books, 2015.

6.2 Secondary Sources

Bloom, Allan. *Shakespeare on Love and Friendship*. Chicago: U of Chicago P, 2000.

Bradby, G. F. *The Problems of Hamlet*. London: Oxford UP, 1928.

Burre, Herbert. *Das Freundschaftsmotiv und seine Abwandlung in den Dramen Shakespeares*. Ph.D. dissertation, Philosophische Fakultät, Philipps Universität Marburg, 1938.

Dakin, Marry Ellen. "Introduction: 'To the Great Variety of Readers'" *Reading Shakespeare with Young Adults*. n.p.: Natl Council of Teachers of English, 2011. xv

Hornby, Albert Sydney. "Adder". *Oxford Advanced Learner's Dictionary of Current English*. Eds. Margaret Deuter et al., 9th ed., Cornelsen, 2015. 17

Marx, Peter. *Hamlet-Handbuch: Stoffe, Aneignungen, Deutungen*. Weimar: J. B. Metzler, 2014. 42

Wilson, John Dover. *What happens in Hamlet*. 1935. Cambridge: Cambridge UP, 1956.

6.3 Webliography

Bratberg, Terje. "Rosenkrantz" Store Norske Leksikon. Feb. 6th, 2016.
<https://snl.no/Rosenkrantz>, (accessed Nov. 5th, 2018).

Bratberg, Terje. "Gyldenstierne" Store Norske Leksikon. Feb. 14th, 2009.
<https://snl.no/Gyldenstierne>, (accessed Nov. 5th, 2018).

New International Version. Biblica, 2011. BibleGateway.com,
<https://www.biblegateway.com/passage/?search=John+20&version=NIV>,
(accessed Nov. 5th, 2018).

The University of Chicago. Harper Lecture with David Bevington: Love and Friendship in
Hamlet. Online video clip. YouTube. YouTube, Nov. 29th, 2012.
(accessed Nov. 5th, 2018).

Tosh, Will. "Shakespeare and Friendship". The British Library. 2015.
<https://www.bl.uk/shakespeare/articles/shakespeare-and-friendship>,
(accessed Nov. 5th, 2018).

6.4 Illustration Directory

Illustration 1 (page 4): Wither, George. "Book 4: Illustration XXIX." *A Collection of
Emblemes, ancient and modern: quickened with metricall Illustrations, both morall
and divine.* London. 1635. 237
<https://publicdomainreview.org/collections/george-withersemblem-book-1635/>,
(accessed Nov. 5th, 2018).

7 Appendix

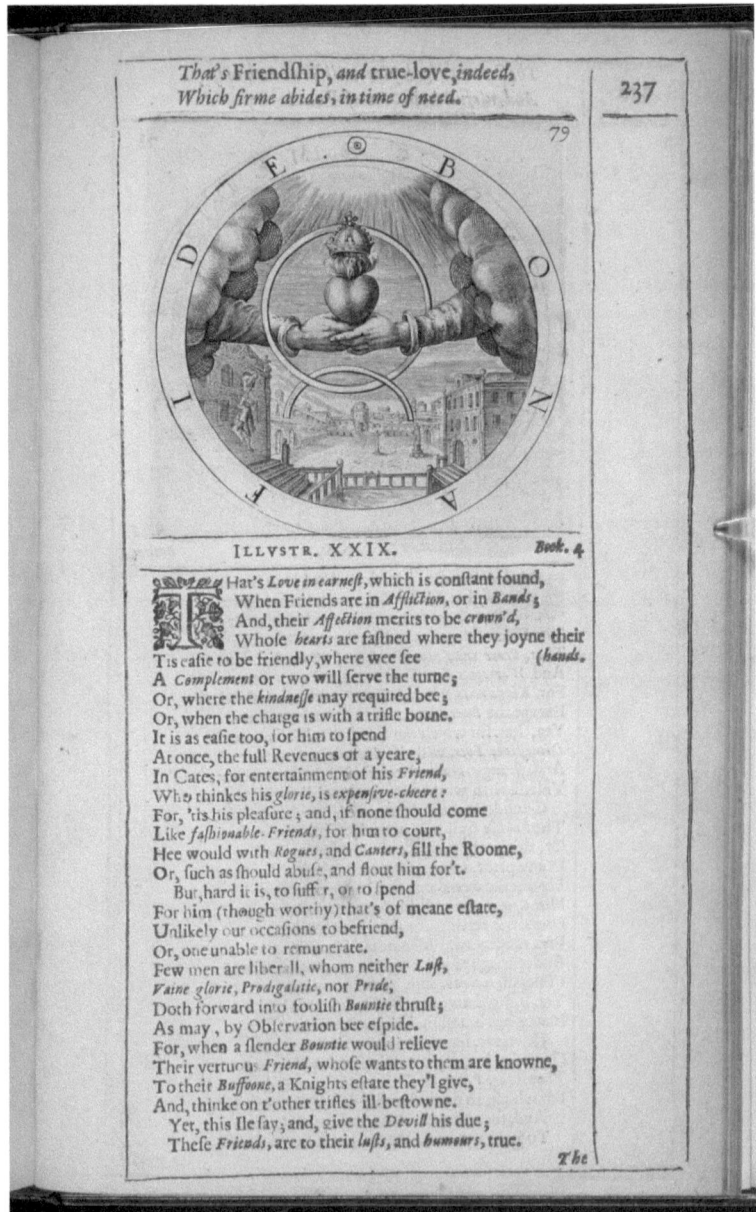

That's Friendſhip, *and* true-love, *indeed,*
Which ſirme abides, *in time of need.*

237

79

ILLVSTR. XXIX.   *Book.* 4.

Hat's *Love in earneſt,* which is conſtant found,
When Friends are in *Affliction,* or in *Bands;*
And, their *Affection* merits to be *crown'd,*
Whoſe *hearts* are faſtned where they joyne their
Tis eaſie to be friendly, where wee ſee   (*hands.*
A *Complement* or two will ſerve the turne;
Or, where the *kindneſſe* may required bee;
Or, when the charge is with a trifle borne.
It is as eaſie too, for him to ſpend
At once, the full Revenues of a yeare,
In Cates, for entertainment of his *Friend,*
Who thinkes his *glorie,* is *expenſive-cheere:*
For, 'tis his pleaſure; and, if none ſhould come
Like *faſhionable- Friends,* for him to court,
Hee would with *Rogues,* and *Canters,* fill the Roome,
Or, ſuch as ſhould abuſe, and flout him for't.
  But, hard it is, to ſuffer, or to ſpend
For him (though worthy) that's of meane eſtate,
Unlikely our occaſions to befriend,
Or, one unable to remunerate.
Few men are liberall, whom neither *Luſt,*
Vaine glorie, Prodigalitie, nor *Pride,*
Doth forward into fooliſh *Bountie* thruſt;
As may, by Obſervation bee eſpide.
For, when a ſlender *Bountie* would relieve
Their vertuous *Friend,* whoſe wants to them are knowne,
To their *Buffoone,* a Knights eſtate they'l give,
And, thinke on t'other trifles ill-beſtowne.
  Yet, this Ile ſay; and, give the *Devill* his due;
Theſe *Friends,* are to their *luſts,* and *humours,* true.

The

Illustration 1: Friendship in George Wither's emblem book